The Peter F. [...]
for Nonprofit Management

HOW TO ASSESS YOUR NONPROFIT ORGANIZATION WITH PETER DRUCKER'S FIVE MOST IMPORTANT QUESTIONS

User Guide for Boards, Staff, Volunteers, and Facilitators

DEVELOPED BY

Constance Rossum

THE DRUCKER FOUNDATION SELF-ASSESSMENT TOOL FOR NONPROFIT ORGANIZATIONS

Jossey-Bass Publishers   San Francisco

The
Jossey-Bass
Nonprofit Sector
Series

Substantial discounts on bulk quantities of Jossey-Bass books
are available to corporations, professional associations, and other
organizations. For details and discount information, contact the
special sales department at Jossey-Bass Inc., Publishers.
(415) 433-1740; Fax (415) 433-0499.

For international orders, please contact your local Paramount Publishing
International office.

Manufactured in the United States of America

Manufactured in the United States of America. Nearly all Jossey-Bass
books and jackets are printed on recycled paper that contains at least
50 percent recycled waste, including 10 percent postconsumer waste.
Many of our materials are also printed with vegetable-based ink; during
the printing process these inks emit fewer volatile organic compounds
(VOCs) than petroleum-based inks. VOCs contribute to the formation of
smog.

ISBN: 1–55542–596–8
LC: 93–37810

FIRST EDITION
PB Printing 10 9 8 7 6 5 4

Code 9398

CONTENTS

FOREWORD

"You say we should achieve excellence, but how do we know when we get there?" was the most compelling message our brand new foundation heard in the fall of 1990 as we began our work. This *Self-Assessment Tool* is our response.

The *Drucker Foundation Self-Assessment Tool* presents a process for *organizational* self-assessment, not for *program* evaluation or *individual* performance appraisal. It provides a framework for addressing the important questions: "What is our mission?" "How are we doing?" "Are we heading in the right direction?"

It is designed, though, to be used in the most appropriate way for your organization. There is no best way; you use and adapt it to the needs and culture of your organization. Make it your own. Many organizations will use the *Tool* with discussion groups of members with a facilitator from within or outside the organization, supplementing those discussion groups with interviews of the board and staff leaders; other organizations will use it in different ways. For example, the *Tool* can be used by the leadership team of an organization: the chairperson of the board and the chief executive officer. The *Tool* can be used by a management or officer team, or by a small group assessing its progress. The *Tool* can also be used by an individual who desires to clarify his or her understanding of the organization's mission and performance.

When an organization chooses to use the *Drucker Foundation Self-Assessment Tool*, one team plays a unique role. The leadership team, comprising the board chairperson and the chief executive officer, has the critical responsibility of overseeing the organization's self-assessment. The chairperson recommends to the board that the self-assessment be undertaken. The chief executive officer directs the process from beginning to end, ensuring that the aims and expectations for the self-assessment are known by those participating in it and facilitating it. The leadership team receives the final report of discussion groups and interviews and is responsible for disseminating the findings and leading the organization in the action required.

We hope you will see self-assessment as an integral part of your organization's planning system and as part of an ongoing process of organizational renewal. In preparation for the intellectual and emotional adventure—for hearts and minds are involved—background material for the discussion groups and interviews may be needed. Depending on the circumstances, this material might include internal data on membership, services delivered, structure and deployment of people and allocation of resources; environmental scanning, with major trends identified that may affect the organization, and the implication of those trends; publications, annual reports, and any communication tools that provide background for the discussion; other information about the organization, its constituents, and its community.

This is a unique tool. Many volunteers and staff and numerous organizations have been involved in the development and testing of the *Self-Assessment Tool*, but at its core is the management philosophy of Peter F. Drucker.

If you could invite Peter Drucker to visit your nonprofit organization and sit down with your board and management team, these are the five questions he would ask you to answer:

- What is our business (mission)?
- Who is our customer?
- What does the customer consider value?
- What have been our results?
- What is our plan?

The *Tool* embodies the process he uses in his consultations with nonprofit organizations. In the *Workbook*, Drucker speaks to participants in his own direct language of management and leadership. He provides practical guidance on assessing your mission, understanding your customers, measuring your performance, and planning for action.

The Drucker questions are the fundamental questions all of us must be able to answer if, indeed, we are to change lives and build community, if we are to be true to our mission, achieve our goals, and manage for results. It is our hope that this *Self-Assessment Tool* will be a helpful and friendly guide on your organization's journey to excellence.

July 1993

Frances Hesselbein
President
The Peter F. Drucker Foundation
for Nonprofit Management

ABOUT PETER F. DRUCKER

Peter F. Drucker is a writer, teacher, and consultant. Recognized as the father of modern management, he has helped to revolutionize this field in both theory and practice, through his career as a professor of politics, philosophy, and management.

As a management consultant Peter Drucker specializes in economic and business policy and in top management organization. For over fifty years he has consulted with organizations in the private, governmental, and nonprofit sectors in the United States and abroad.

Drucker's work with nonprofit organizations includes consulting with small and large organizations in fields ranging from the arts to health care, from refugee services to religious organizations to youth organizations. Since 1990, when his *Managing the Non-Profit Organization* was published, he has served as honorary chairman of The Peter F. Drucker Foundation for Nonprofit Management.

His first book, *The End of Economic Man*, was published in 1939. His management books—*The Practice of Management* (1954), *The Effective Executive* (1966), *Management: Tasks; Responsibilities; Practices* (1974), *Managing Turbulent Times* (1980), *Innovation and Entrepreneurship* (1985), and others—are international best-sellers and have been translated into more than twenty languages. His twenty-seventh book, *Post-Capitalist Society*, was published in 1993.

In addition to writing books, Drucker has been a frequent contributor to various magazines and journals over the years and is an editorial columnist for the *Wall Street Journal*.

Drucker was born in 1909 in Vienna and was educated there and in England. He took his doctorate in public and international law while working as a newspaper reporter in Frankfurt, Germany, and then worked as an economist for an international bank in London. He came to the United States in 1937. He began his teaching career as professor of politics and philosophy at Bennington College; for more than twenty years he was professor of management at the Graduate Business School of New York University. Since 1971, he has been Clarke Professor of Social Science and Management at Claremont Graduate School.

Drucker has four children and six grandchildren. A hiker and student of Japan and Japanese art, he lives with his wife Doris in Claremont, California.

ABOUT THE
PETER F. DRUCKER FOUNDATION
FOR NONPROFIT MANAGEMENT

The Peter F. Drucker Foundation for Nonprofit Management was founded in 1990. Named for and guided by the acknowledged father of modern management, its mission is to *help the social sector achieve excellence in performance and build responsible citizenship*.

By providing educational opportunities and resources to the leadership of nonprofit organizations, the Drucker Foundation aims to *inspire* and *enable* those leaders to realize the full potential of their organizations. It pursues these goals through the presentation of conferences, video teleconferences, and the annual Peter F. Drucker Award for Nonprofit Innovation, as well as through the development of management resources and publications for nonprofit boards, staff, and volunteers.

For More Information:

If you would like more information on the Drucker Foundation and its programs or would like to share your thoughts on the *Self-Assessment Tool*, please write or fax us at the address given below.

We are very interested in your experience using our *Self-Assessment Tool*, and we welcome your comments and evaluations. Tell us about your experience using the *Tool*, the results it produced in your organization, or anything else you think is important.

Your comments and suggestions will help us to refine the *Tool* in future editions. We are also interested in your suggestions on other tools, publications, and resources that would be valuable to you and your nonprofit organization. Your comments will help us to offer better service to you and your nonprofit colleagues.

We welcome your participation; please send your requests for information and comments to

The Drucker Foundation
666 Fifth Avenue, 10th Floor
New York, NY 10103
Tel: 212-399-1710
Fax: 212-399-4426

ACKNOWLEDGMENTS

We are deeply grateful to Constance Rossum of Management Directives, Inc. for her development of the *Self-Assessment Tool* process and format as well as her coordination and facilitation of focus groups and field tests. Her work transformed the thinking and writings of Peter F. Drucker into a practical tool for nonprofit organizations.

The development and production of this *Tool* were dependent on the assistance given by many individuals. They represented their organization and themselves, and gave comments on the text and process, participated in test assessments, and provided encouragement and criticism. Among the many who helped were Lillie Branch, Cathleen Brown, Olwen Brown, Robert Buford, Marguerite Carlsen, Clint Clampitt, Steve Deitsch, Betty Ann Dillon, Doris Drucker, Myrna Elliott, Linda Foreman, C. Worth George, Barbara Gibson, Gary Glenney, Karen Green, Frederick G. Harmon, Karen Hinton, Richard Hogan, Joseph C. Schreiber II, Karen Johnson, Robert W. Johnston, Robert Kramer, Rich Leary, Georgia McManigal, Deidre Moulliet, Candra Parker-Barr, Tom Paterson, Norm Purdue, Tyrus C. Ragland, Ralph A. Rossum, Richard F. Schubert, Alan Shrader, Mike Still, Faith Stein, Margo Sullivan, and David Trickett.

The following organizations provided assistance through their representatives who reviewed or tested the materials for the *Tool*. For their participation, we thank the American Cancer Society, Burke Bases, Casa Colina Foundation, Chaffey College Foundation, Claremont McKenna College, Commonwealth Girl Scout Council, Jefferson Circle, Jossey-Bass Publishers, Leadership Network, Literacy Council of Metro Richmond, Message Factors, Inc., Multiple Sclerosis Society of Southern California,

Navigators, Pathfinders, Pilgrim Place, Planes of Fame Museum, Points of Light Foundation, Sonoma County Volunteer Center, Synthesis Consulting, Visiting Nurse Association of Pomona West End, Inc., and World Vision.

Special thanks are extended to Peggy Haskin of Clerical Services Unlimited and to Sharon Silvia for their support in the typing of interviews, transcripts, and focus group and field test reports. We also thank the hundreds of nonprofit board members and executives who participated in our national video teleconference. Their questions and comments provided valuable information as we developed the *Tool*. Thanks are extended to members of the Drucker Foundation Board of Governors: Robert Buford, chairman; Richard F. Schubert, vice chairman; John A. McNeice, Jr., treasurer; Sidney E. Harris; and John E. Jacob. They were generous with their time, advice, support, and encouragement throughout the development of this publication. Our final thanks go to the Foundation's honorary chairman, Peter F. Drucker, for his decades of dedication to the effective organization, for his contributions to management literature and this *Tool*, and for his support and contributions to the social sector.

Frances Hesselbein
New York, New York

THE FIVE DRUCKER QUESTIONS

1. What Is Our Business (Mission)?

2. Who Is Our Customer?

3. What Does the Customer Consider Value?

4. What Have Been Our Results?

5. What Is Our Plan?

WHY SELF-ASSESSMENT?
by Peter F. Drucker

Good Intentions Are Not Enough

The ninety million volunteers who work for nonprofit institutions—America's largest employer—exemplify the American commitment to responsible citizenship in the community. Indeed, nonprofit organizations are central to the quality of life in America and are its most distinguishing feature.

Forty years ago *management* was a very bad word in nonprofit organizations. Management meant *business*, and the one thing a nonprofit was not was a *business*. Today, nonprofits understand that they need management all the more because they have no conventional bottom line. Now they need to learn how to use management so they can concentrate on their mission. Yet, there are few tools available that address the distinct characteristics and central needs of the many nonprofit organizations in America.

Although I don't know a single for-profit business that is as well managed as a few of the nonprofits, the great majority of the nonprofits can be graded a "C" at best. Not for lack of effort; most of them work very hard. But for lack of *focus*, and for lack of *tool competence*. I predict that this will change, however, and we at the Drucker Foundation hope to make our greatest impact in these areas of focus and tool competence.

For years, most nonprofits felt that good intentions were by themselves enough. But today, we know that because we don't have a bottom line, we have to manage *better* than for-profit business. We have to have discipline rooted in our mission. We have to manage our limited resources of people and money for maximum effectiveness. And we have to think through very clearly what results are for our organization.

Why This Tool Was Developed

When we announced in 1990 that we were establishing The Peter F. Drucker Foundation for Nonprofit Management, many in the nonprofit sector approached me, Frances Hesselbein, and some of our board members, saying, "The most important management resource we need is a method to help us think through what we are doing, why we are doing it, and how we are doing it. The big, national nonprofits are able to do this. But groups like us—a small battered women's shelter, for example—need something that we can do with our own people without having to call in a consultant, something that motivates and stimulates us." And so we at the Foundation listened to our customers and set our priorities.

During the past year, we've developed and tested our *Self-Assessment Tool*. I've tested it as well with my own nonprofit friends. It works. The most important aspect of the *Self-Assessment Tool* is the questions it poses. Answers are important; you need answers because you need action. But the most important thing is to ask these questions.

Self-assessment was the subject of the Drucker Foundation's recent national teleconference. About a third of the participants who completed the *Tool* prior to the conference told me that it was a very painful exercise, that they discovered that they don't agree among themselves. And I said, "Hurray." One purpose of self-assessment is to find out that there are decisions to be made. There are legitimate grounds for disagreement on priorities.

For example, one organization that used the *Tool* said it revealed major differences in opinion among their membership on key issues. About half the members believed they should start centers in other cities, and half believed the contrary—that they should concentrate first on building a model center in one city. Now, that difference requires a very critical and important decision because you can do *only* one or the other with your resources. But if you don't bring out these kinds of questions in the context of self-assessment, you will have constant friction within your organization.

Focus on Mission—Learn to Say No

This *Self-Assessment Tool* forces an organization to focus on its mission. About eight out of ten nonprofits in the country are small organizations whose leaders find it very hard to say no when someone comes to them with a good cause. I advised some close friends of mine, working with a local council of churches, that half the things they are doing they shouldn't be doing—not because they're unimportant but because they're not needed. I told them, "Other people can do those activities and do them well. Maybe a few years ago it was a good idea for you to help get this farmers' market started because those Vietnamese farmers in your area needed a place to sell their produce; but it's going well now, and you don't have to run it anymore. It's time for organized abandonment."

Encouraging Constructive Dissent

Over the years, I've learned that constructive dissent can be used effectively. For example, perhaps you have a colleague who is very strongly opposed to taking a certain action that you feel should be taken. By using the *Self-Assessment Tool*, you are forced to listen to each other. And suddenly you understand each other. Dissent is emotional, not rational, and it is aggravated by misinformation. By asking the question, "What are the facts?" the *Tool* helps us understand that we are all trying to accomplish the same thing. We are committed to the same mission.

The *Self-Assessment Tool* Strengthens the Strategic Planning Process

The *Drucker Foundation Self-Assessment Tool* will help you focus on certain aspects of the strategic planning process; in fact, it provides the platform for successful planning because it combines strategic planning and performance evaluation with a focus on results. It asks, "*Where* do we need *what* action, and *who* is going to do *what*?"

During self-assessment, you ask, "Why are we here?" "What is the mission?" And "What is the mission?" is always the first question you should ask during strategic planning. However, most plans I see don't ask it; they take for granted that you already know the answer. So, in the *Self-Assessment Tool*, we ask the questions, "Where do we put our resources?" "What things work?" "What things would work if we took them seriously enough?" "What should be abandoned?" "Where have we become lax?" "Where have we become complacent and smug?"

The *Self-Assessment Tool* is an integral part of the strategic planning process. It strengthens the process because in strategic planning you rarely ask, "What are we doing well?" "How well should we be doing?" The *Self-Assessment Tool* melds into one process strategic planning and effective performance.

How to Begin

I invite you now to join your colleagues in the creative process of self-assessment. You can work together as missionaries to achieve your organization's most important goals.

July 1993

Peter F. Drucker
Claremont, California

The *Drucker Foundation Self-Assessment Tool* is a results oriented, strategic thinking process designed as a management resource for nonprofit organizations and their members. Initially developed for small and midsize nonprofit organizations, the *Self-Assessment Tool* has also been used successfully by major nonprofit organizations as a supplement to their existing evaluation and planning processes. It is based on Peter F. Drucker's principles of effective management that have been utilized over the past half century by successful for-profit *and* nonprofit organizations. The *Self-Assessment Tool* helps nonprofits focus on Drucker's five critical management questions: What is our business (mission)? Who is our customer? What does the customer consider value? What have been our results? What is our plan?

The *Self-Assessment Tool*

- Is easy to use and easy to complete within a short period of time
- Clearly explains and demonstrates Peter F. Drucker's management principles and their application to nonprofit organizations
- Encourages diverse participation within the organization
- Forces clarity of thinking by asking participants to define their organization's mission, customers, values, and results
- Supplements the organization's existing strategic planning and evaluation processes

- Focuses on results by requiring clearly defined goals and a realistic plan to achieve them and by emphasizing roles, responsibilities, and ongoing measurement and assessment
- Reduces dependence on outside consultants for strategic planning and evaluation

The *Self-Assessment Tool* encourages participation from diverse groups throughout the nonprofit organization—from the board chairperson and the chief executive officer to volunteers, staff, donors, members, and the customers it serves. This simple but effective *Self-Assessment Tool* has been tested and refined by representative nonprofit organizations and by marketing and research experts whose comments on the process—the outline, methodology, facilitation, and analytical outcome—were critical to its development.

A nonprofit executive described the value of the *Drucker Foundation Self-Assessment Tool* in this way:

> [It is] a process that doesn't waste our time or talents, one that asks "real" questions, can be done during a reasonable period of time, puts conflict into a workable context, leads to action, allows us to get closure by the end of the process, and doesn't require a lot of homework.

Using the Self-Assessment Components

There are two components in the *Drucker Foundation Self-Assessment Tool*: this *User Guide* and the *Participant's Workbook*.

The User Guide

This guide provides the leaders of nonprofit organizations— the board chairperson, the chief executive, the board members, and the staff—with an overview of the *Drucker Foundation Self-Assessment Tool* and its benefits. It also provides guidelines for selecting a facilitator and participants for the assessment process and discussion groups. It includes "Facilitator Guidelines" that provide instruction on conducting the depth interviews and the discussion groups with participants who have completed the *Workbook*. Its last section—"Discussion Guide for

Facilitators"—presents questions designed to stimulate further discussion during the interviews and discussion groups.

The Participant's Workbook

The workbook is prefaced with instructive observations from Peter F. Drucker regarding the effective management of non-profit organizations. It is, for this reason, more than simply a workbook; it is an instructional text. The *Tool* was tested among participants representing a number of nonprofit organizations including colleges, churches, hospitals, youth groups, and social services. We found that participants enthusiastically read, enjoyed, and took to heart the true-life examples that Drucker used to illustrate each of his five critical management questions. And so this workbook is to a large extent a record of what non-profits need, want, and can use effectively. Because it was developed in response to our customers' needs, it provides information and instruction that *create value for the customers* of the Drucker Foundation for Nonprofit Management.

Our participants told us that they wanted to have in one volume what Peter F. Drucker describes as "the why, the what, and the how." They wanted a workbook that told them story by story what to do, what steps to take, and how to think through the philosophy and basic values underlying this "business" approach. The resulting workbook process, rather than being a cumbersome task, reflects scholarly theory brought to life by Peter Drucker's instruction on each of the five questions.

The five-question outline, which reflects the Drucker principles, is the heart of the *Self-Assessment Tool*. The central component of the *Participant's Workbook*, it is also used as the basis for the group discussions. The introduction to each of the five Drucker questions is followed by worksheets to be completed by the participants before their participation in small group discussions.

The *Participant's Workbook* can be used in a variety of ways (see also the section, "Choosing Participants"). It can be completed independently by the leadership team, the board chairperson, and the chief executive officer as a first step in the self-assessment process; it can be completed independently by the leadership team and followed by a depth interview with an experienced facilitator. Or, it can be completed independently by six to ten representatives at similar levels of authority, such as groups of staff, volunteers, or members of the board, followed by participation in a discussion group session led by a facilitator.

Focusing on Results

During the process of focusing on the five basic questions, nonprofits will clarify their mission and identify their customers and what their customers consider value. At the same time, the process will reveal the areas in which they are less effective and will help them reorganize, refocus, or perhaps even abandon some of their efforts.

The executive director or chief executive officer is best equipped to introduce the *Self-Assessment Tool* as a management resource for the organization. When Peter Drucker is asked the question, "Whose responsibility is it to introduce the *Self-Assessment Tool* into an organization, and how do I get my board to go along with it?" he answers that it is the responsibility of the executive to say, "Let's look at what we are doing."

While a facilitator guides the group through the self-assessment process, it is the participants who will ultimately determine—or at least question—what they should be doing and define the next steps needed to achieve their goals. Some incorrect information will surface and some goal conflict should be expected—especially if several discussion groups and depth interviews are conducted during the self-assessment process. These events should be viewed as a healthy exchange of ideas and opinions, and each final report is written to reflect the range of the group's opinions. It is the facilitator's role to write and present the final report to the leadership team, who then review and disseminate the findings, determine the next steps, and develop an implementation plan for the organization.

Applying Business Terms to Nonprofits

The nonprofit organization has no "bottom line"; rather, it focuses on making a difference in society and in changing the life of the individual. Therefore, nonprofits need to understand and to use proven business terms to help them identify their mission and to focus on activities that will achieve results. They can use business vocabulary to help them become more effective. The *Self-Assessment Tool* uses words like *mission, customer, value,* and *results*. Because some members of your organization may be uncomfortable with these words, we provide the following definitions for them to consider as they complete the *Participant's Workbook*.

Mission.   The mission is your organization's reason for being. It is the end result you want the organization to achieve. It defines why you do what you do, and its ultimate goal is to mobilize the organization's human resources to get the right things done.

Customers.   Customers are people who can choose to accept or reject your services, membership in your organization, and so on. They have to be seen as people who must be satisfied. All non-profit organizations have more than one type of customer: the *primary customers* (those who use the service), and the *supporting customers* (volunteers, donors, members of the community, the board, and the staff).

Value.   Whether you are developing programs, recruiting volunteers, or soliciting donations, you should look at what your *customers* value. All of your customers must want what you deliver. Value for your customers answers the question: "What of the things we do—or can do—for you really helps you?" As Drucker says: "If they don't put your service to use, if they don't want what you offer them, you are working in vain."

Results.   Results are what the organization has achieved as defined by the mission. Once the mission is defined, you must translate it into action—into specific goals, objectives, and action steps.

Choosing Participants

The *Drucker Foundation Self-Assessment Tool* provides opportunities for participation at all levels of the organization.

Participants should be selected from among those who are willing to commit the necessary time, and they should include strategic thinkers as well as those who tend to be more task oriented. Both kinds of thinkers are important to create balance between time spent on generating and exploring ideas and time spent in translating ideas into action.

The executive director or chief executive officer and other senior staff may complete the *Participant's Workbook* independently, followed by a depth interview with the facilitator. In our experience, the nonprofit staff leaders, given their unique perspectives, benefit more from a one-on-one interview with the facilitator than from participation in a discussion group. Moreover, including staff leaders in a group consisting of individuals occupying various levels of responsibility may affect the outcome if some group members perceive them as authority figures.

Board members should also be encouraged to complete the *Participant's Workbook* independently and participate in a discussion group with other board members. (The board chairperson, however, should participate in the one-on-one depth interview sequence.)

Volunteers and staff who represent the organization at similar levels of responsibility may complete the *Participant's Workbook* independently, then join a discussion group to share experiences. Within each discussion group, participants may represent a range of experience, geographic regions, programs, ages, racial and ethnic groups, both sexes, and so on. This mix will contribute to the diversity of ideas and experiences. This diversity gives the organization the best opportunity to examine itself honestly; few understand better than the grass roots volunteers and staff the customers' needs and the areas in which the organization is or is not effective.

Using the Workbook

Before the potential participants begin the process, they should be brought together by the leadership to meet the facilitator and to review the *Self-Assessment Tool* so that everyone understands why the organization is using it, as well as its specific objectives and methodology. Participants also need to understand their roles, the expected results, and how their group participation will fit into the total process. Again, it is important that participants understand the significant time commitment required to ensure success.

The *Participant's Workbook* provides worksheets for each question, organized so that the participants can take notes and record ideas at their own pace. Each area detailed in the five-question outline is preceded by observations by Peter F. Drucker, who shares his many experiences with nonprofits in a simple, straightforward, and conversational tone. The workbook is not collected or "graded" in any way; it is for the participant's personal use only. However, the participants are encouraged to bring the completed worksheets to the discussion session, as the questions asked in the workbook address the same areas that will be covered in depth during the discussion or interview sessions.

All participants—from the leadership team through volunteers and staff—should begin by reading the workbook's introduction to self-assessment by Peter F. Drucker and reviewing the five basic questions in the outline. Next, they should review the workbook format. (This step will take about one hour.) Finally, they should plan on spending an additional three to five hours completing the worksheets and collecting information from other sources. We recommend that this be done the week prior to the discussion sessions. It is critical that participants understand and be willing to commit the amount of time involved in the total process.

Understanding the Facilitator's Role

Selecting an effective facilitator is key to the success of the self-assessment process. Whether facilitators are selected from inside or outside the organization, their role is to guide the group discussion in a nondirective manner to ensure that all areas of the Drucker outline are thoroughly covered, to include the discussion of other relevant issues that may arise during the session, and to prevent the group from getting off the track. Facilitators must also encourage all participants to participate fully in the discussion. They are responsible for writing the report, recording the proposed implementation plan for each session, and communicating the results to the leadership team.

If possible, the same facilitator should be used for all discussion groups or depth interviews conducted within an organization during a given time period. The advantages of using a single facilitator are continuity and depth of analysis; the facilitator can encourage additional interaction with each subsequent group or with all interviewees by asking them to react to what was said in the previous group or interview. If an organization has many participants, necessitating multiple groups, facilitator teams can be used. All facilitators are then equally responsible for the facilitation process and for writing the final report.

The facilitator tape-records the discussion group sessions and depth interviews to review for later analysis and to use as a guide for writing the report.

Choosing a Facilitator

The facilitator—whether from within or outside the organization—needs to invest some time in developing a comfortable familiarity with the five-question outline and the *Participant's Workbook*. Additionally, the facilitator should

- Be results focused, understand clearly what is to be accomplished during the session, and communicate it often to the group

- Be a good listener. The Drucker questions are clearly outlined; however, the facilitator must listen closely to all discussion, ask related questions, probe for clarity, challenge inconsistent statements, and ask for reactions to other interpretations from previous groups or depth interviews

- Be able to exercise control while encouraging participation. Each group will have its talkers and its shy or more reserved participants. The facilitator should keep the discussion moving among all participants and know when and how to discourage those who would monopolize the discussion and how to encourage others to share their points of view.

- Be an analytic and strategic thinker who can communicate the results of the discussion orally and in writing

- Be perceived by participants as impartial and trustworthy.

Those choosing facilitators often view their primary role as that of a pleasant conversationalist or as a group moderator whose function is simply to keep the discussion moving. Others believe that if facilitators are conducting the group, they will be too busy to think about notetaking and analysis and will therefore require a co-facilitator to take notes or write the report. This has not been our experience. Because facilitators must always be focused on the end result they want to achieve with the group, they must frame and ask questions that will enable them to communicate results orally and in writing for the participants and the leadership team. The audio-taped interviews serve as a necessary record of discussion for the facilitator's report.

Sources of Outside Facilitators

If a qualified facilitator is unavailable within your organization or you would prefer a facilitator from outside, there are many sources that can provide assistance. You may secure recommendations for pro bono or reduced-fee outside facilitators from local organizations that support nonprofit organizations and the community. These include organizations that provide technical and management support, organizations that offer consulting services, organizations that support volunteer efforts, organizations of retired executives, and academic organizations including colleges, universities, business schools, and community colleges. Representatives of these organizations may provide their own services or recommend others.

Facilitators who specialize in strategic planning for nonprofit and for-profit organizations may also be recommended by members of your board of directors who are familiar with the quality of their work in similar areas.

As noted earlier, the organization must feel confident that the facilitator is both knowledgeable and credible; that is, he or she understands both the Drucker *Tool* and the process of group discussion, and is perceived as unbiased so that the outcome of the process is not affected by what others believe to be the facilitator's personal agenda or that of any internal group or the leadership.

Understandably, an organization with a small, lean staff may find it difficult to commit significant staff time to the assessment process. The time factor, along with facilitation and analytical skills and credibility, are the major reasons some organizations seek a facilitator who is outside the organization.

The facilitator should be chosen carefully as this relationship requires a significant commitment on both sides and can affect the future direction and success of the organization.

Applying Discussion Groups to Self-Assessment

The discussion group process is characterized by *interaction*. All participants are encouraged to share their ideas and to respond, question, and agree or disagree fully with each other. This interaction helps the organization identify and clarify important areas of concern, needs, or opportunity, and to uncover incorrect information that may exist.

In our experience, most discussion group sessions using the *Self-Assessment Tool* can be completed in three to four hours. Some organizations like to set aside a full day, with a follow-up session scheduled later. Others schedule their sessions as a board or staff retreat. Still others rely on evening sessions with volunteer groups. The flexibility of the *Self-Assessment Tool* accommodates these various uses. The length of time required depends on the needs and complexity of issues within the organization.

Focusing on "Self"-Assessment

Although the facilitator is important, the focus of the *Tool* is on "self"-assessment. The role of the facilitator is critical in guiding the group through the self-assessment process and in making sure all questions are thoroughly covered, important peripheral areas are addressed, and the results of the process are achieved. But self-assessment without *interaction* and *action in the form of next steps* is likely to be all exercise and little result.

Finally, the role of the facilitator is *not* to make policy or to manipulate the outcome. The discussion content, and therefore the substance and results of the self-assessment, depends on the selection, preparation, and follow-up by the organization's participants and its leadership.

FACILITATOR GUIDELINES

Your Role as Facilitator

Your primary role is that of project director and your objective is to guide all the various participants—from the board chairperson and chief executive officer to the volunteer groups and staff—through the *Drucker Foundation Self-Assessment Tool*, to help them answer questions designed to make them and their organization more effective, and to help them begin to develop a plan to achieve their organization's goals. This is a serious but rewarding undertaking to which you must be willing to devote considerable preparation time. You will need to understand the project objectives and to familiarize yourself with the Drucker principles, the five-question outline, and the *Participant's Workbook*, as well as the needs of the organization.

Preparing for the Project

Regardless of your experience, the following activities will help you prepare for this project.

- Carefully read this *User Guide* so you understand the perspective of nonprofit leadership.

- If you are unfamiliar with the organization for which you will facilitate, ask the executive director to supply background information about it.

- Arrange to meet with the organization's leadership team to clarify issues and discuss background information. This meeting may also reveal special vocabulary or concerns that could arise during the discussion sessions.

- Make sure that you have a clear understanding of your charge in terms of the scope of the self-assessment you are facilitating. Are you being asked to assist in assessing overall organizational performance, including the organization's basic mission? Or, are you looking at one program area, or perhaps a group or other organizational unit? Self-assessment can be conducted on various levels, so it is important to clarify expectations.

- Work with the board-staff leadership to help select participants and determine project scope if requested.

- Review the list of participants prior to each discussion group and depth interview so that you understand each person's job function and responsibilities.

- Carefully study the five questions of the *Drucker Foundation Self-Assessment Tool* and the "Discussion Guide for Facilitators" on pages 22–34. The five-question outline may appear at first to be a simple series of questions, but it is important that you think through the five Drucker questions and their application to the worksheets that follow them in the *Participant's Workbook*. As facilitator, you may also need to devise additional relevant questions that may help clarify issues and identify potential areas of conflict. You should feel comfortable with the discussion group objectives and the *Tool's* business terms so that you can frame each of your questions effectively.

- Finally, review and complete the worksheets in the *Participant's Workbook*. Answer the questions for this nonprofit organization as if you were a discussion group participant.

Whether you are a novice facilitator or one who has conducted numerous group discussions or depth interviews, the following will answer general questions you may have about facilitation and your specific questions about the *Self-Assessment Tool*.

Beginning the Session

After introducing yourself to the discussion group participants, begin your introduction with an explanation of the *Drucker Foundation Self-Assessment Tool* and the discussion group process; then explain what the group needs to accomplish during the three- to four-hour session. Include a brief description of Peter F.

Drucker's work in the business and nonprofit sectors and the purpose of the Drucker Foundation. Prior to the group discussion, explain the following points:

- A discussion group involves free-flowing interaction. Unlike a serial interview, you do not ask participants to give their opinions in turn around the table. Instead, they can jump into the discussion when they have something to contribute or if they want to pose a question to you or to the other participants.

- There are no flip charts or other visual aids because it is important that you and the participants focus on the five Drucker questions without interruption, and that everyone listen to one another.

- Except for factual data such as number of volunteers, there are no right or wrong answers. Participants are free to agree or disagree with one another or to ask each other questions.

- Participants should speak one at a time and address all comments to the group (rather than to each other) so that you and they can hear what each has to say.

- The session will be tape-recorded to help you recall important issues and comments as you write the final report. If needed, explain to participants that the tapes or transcripts are only for your use and that they will not be reviewed by others in the organization.

- The session will conclude with you and the group working together to complete questions four and five of the outline, that is, evaluating the results of the organization and the group or area for which the participants have responsibility, and recommending a plan.

- Within two to three weeks of the session, you will provide the board chairperson and chief executive officer with a written report that summarizes the sessions and that the leadership team will share with all participants.

Using the Five-Question Outline Effectively

First, review the definitions of key terms—*mission, customer, value, results*—as they apply to nonprofits.

Then, begin each of the five questions with a brief review of the objectives, the results the group is seeking to achieve, and an overview of the Drucker narrative and the question areas addressed in the worksheets.

Before moving to the next section, summarize for the group what you have heard and ask for clarification if needed. Determine at that point what agreements or decisions have been made and what other information is required so that you and the group will be ready to develop your action plan in question five.

Repeat these procedures for each of the five questions. Feel free to return to a section as often as needed to add other comments and encourage participants to revisit any of the five questions or to ask related questions any time during the discussion.

To complete the self-assessment process, it is critical to cover all five questions in detail. However, it is also important to encourage participants to raise related issues that they feel should be covered, such as current fund-raising, recruitment, delivery of services, and so on. Experienced facilitators are encouraged to use their own successful questioning techniques to help the group work through the process.

It is important to remind participants that their self-assessment should focus not only on their perceptions of the entire organization but also on their own areas of familiarity and responsibility. At the same time, encourage participants to offer their observations and perceptions of the results, activities, challenges, or concerns outside their own areas.

By the end of the session, the group will have completed the process and be ready to focus on results and a workable plan. The extent of the plan will differ greatly by organization and individual group.

Using Other Helpful Techniques

While each group will be different, the following general procedures may be helpful.

Don't Rush Through the Five-Question Outline

Avoid the tendency to use the facilitator's "Discussion Guide" as a check-off list for the responses to each question without clarifying the meaning or utility of the question. Remember, the

"Discussion Guide" is a tool that you can use or modify to help the group understand what is needed to achieve results. You can encourage discussion among the participants by asking if anyone else has a comment or agrees or disagrees with a response. Or, ask if there are other important areas to discuss that have not yet been addressed. You can also ask whether anyone needs to revisit or add to questions and issues already addressed.

Encourage Participants to Be Specific and to Give Examples

Challenge participants to explain why or to what extent they feel strongly about a particular issue. Their examples will force meaning and provide a degree of concern, ensuring that both you and the participants will understand better what has been said and what needs to be done. Moreover, when you challenge participants to explain a point of view or reasons for their concern, their ability or inability to articulate the problem can be used as an effective example in the written analysis.

Preparing a Written Report

Your role as facilitator includes working with discussion group and depth interview participants to summarize the results of each session and to report the next steps.

In general, the standard report format includes these areas:

- Background/Historical Perspective
- Methodology
- Objectives
- Description of Participants
- Summary of Findings
- Discussion and Implications for Each of the Five Drucker Questions
- Agreements Reached/Decisions Made During the Session
- Next Steps

The final report should include descriptive verbatim quotations and specific examples as appropriate. Do not, however, substitute a list of participant comments or activities for an analytic point of view. You need to analyze the discussion and results, using the direct quotations to support the findings.

In the report context, the names of the discussion group participants may remain confidential. The transcript and quotations generally are attributed to participants by organization role such as "several recently appointed board members," "members of the senior staff," or "volunteers with more than three years' service."

If multiple discussion group sessions and depth interviews are conducted for a single project, prepare a separate report for each session and then provide an overview of the implications for the nonprofit organization at large. If the multiple discussion groups have more than one facilitator, make sure you work with the other facilitator(s) in writing the report (see "Understanding the Facilitator's Role").

Your efforts will help the organization and its members assess the organization and their roles, and help them become more effective in their work. Approach this project with energy, confidence, and good humor. Your positive attitude, flexibility, and good judgment will contribute significantly to the success of the self-assessment process.

THE DRUCKER FOUNDATION SELF-ASSESSMENT TOOL DISCUSSION GUIDE FOR FACILITATORS

The following pages include the five Drucker questions, the table of contents from the *Participant's Workbook*, and additional questions that might help the facilitator guide the group toward a successful completion of the self-assessment process. These questions support those on the worksheets in the *Participant's Workbook*. In addition, the facilitator is encouraged to add questions relevant to the specific organization.

THE FIVE DRUCKER QUESTIONS

1. What Is Our Business (Mission)?

2. Who Is Our Customer?

3. What Does the Customer Consider Value?

4. What Have Been Our Results?

5. What Is Our Plan?

CONTENTS OF PARTICIPANT'S WORKBOOK

Question 4:   What Have Been Our Results?

Question 5:   What Is Our Plan?

1. What Is Our Business (Mission)?

What Are We Trying to Achieve?

Notes on Mission

a. What specific results are we seeking? For what in the end do we want to be remembered?

b. Do we get adequate results for our efforts? Is this their best allocation?

c. What are our strengths? What have we done well?

d. What are our weaknesses? In what areas do we lack the competence or the resources to be effective?

e. Does our mission statement need to be *refined*? If not, why not? If yes, why is that?

f. In what way, if any, would you rewrite or refocus the mission statement for your organization?

g. What would be the major benefits of the new mission statement? Why do you say that?

h. What problems, if any, would you be likely to encounter with the new mission statement? Among whom? Why is that? What steps, if any, may need to be taken to effect this change?

i. What other questions or issues need to be raised about the mission?

j. What additional information, if any, is needed?

k. What are our next steps?

2. Who Is Our Customer?

What Are We Trying to Achieve?

Notes on Customer

a. Who are our *primary* customers?
   (1) What *value* do we provide each of these customers?
   (2) Do our strengths, our competencies, and resources match the needs of these customers? If yes, in what way? If not, why not?

b. Who are our *supporting* customers both inside and outside the organization?
   (1) What *value* do we provide each of these customers?
   (2) Do our strengths, our competencies, and resources match the needs of these customers? If yes, in what way? If not, why not?

c. In what ways, if any, have our customers *changed*? In terms of
   (1) Demographics? (age, sex, race, ethnicity)
   (2) Primary needs? (training, shelter, day care, and so on)
   (3) Number? (greater, fewer)
   (4) Other ways? (location, workplace, and so on)

d. What are the implications of these changes for our organization?

e. What *other groups* of customers, if any, should we be serving? Why is that?

f. What special competencies does our organization have to benefit them?

2. Who Is Our Customer? *(continued)*

g. What groups of *current* customers are we *not serving well* now? Why is that? (Their needs have changed? Our resources too limited? Other organizations more effective? Their needs do not *fit* our mission? Our competencies?)

h. What groups of current customers, if any, *should we no longer serve?* Why is that?

i. What other questions or issues need to be raised about our customers?

j. What additional information, if any, is needed?

k. What are our next steps?

3. What Does the Customer Consider Value?

What Are We Trying to Achieve?

Notes on Value

a. Think about value in terms of what you and your organization do that fills a specific need, provides satisfaction, or yields a benefit to your customers that they do not receive from another source.

b. How well do we provide what each of our customers considers value? (Review participants' list of customers. Discuss what each considers value and why.)

c. How do we know that?

d. What other questions or issues need to be raised regarding our providing value to our customers?

e. In what ways can we use what our customers consider value to make decisions on
   • Programs (add, enhance, cancel)
   • Recruitment (volunteer skills)
   • Training
   • Fund development
   • Other?

f. What additional information, if any, is needed?

g. What are our next steps?

4. What Have Been Our Results?

How Do We Evaluate Our Work?

Notes on Results

a. How do we define results for our organization? For the group or area for which you have responsibility? How are we measuring them?

b. What in this nonprofit organization (or group) are the *criteria for success?*

c. What are the major goals of *the organization?*

d. To what extent do these goals support the *mission of* the organization? Why or why not?

e. What are the major activities or programs that support these goals?

f. For each key activity, what results do we want to achieve? How do we define results?

g. To what extent have we accomplished these results? Why or why not? How do we know that?

h. Where are our performance strengths? Why is that? How do we know that?

i. In what areas is our work only marginal? Why is that? How do we know that?

j. In what area(s) have we not fulfilled a function, or have reached our objectives and should stop the activity? Why or why not?

k. What additional information is needed to evaluate the results, goals, and activities of this organization?

l. What are the major goals of our specific group/responsibility area?

m. To what extent do our goals support the *mission of the organization?* Why or why not?

n. For each key activity, what results do we want to achieve?

4. What Have Been Our Results? *(continued)*

o. To what extent has our group accomplished its results? Why or why not? How do we know that?

p. Where are our group's performance strengths? Why is that? How do we know that?

q. In what areas is our group's work only marginal? Why is that? How do we know that?

r. In what area(s) has our group not fulfilled a function, or reached our objectives and should stop the activity? Why or why not?

s. What additional information is needed to evaluate the results, goals, and activities of our group/responsibility area?

t. How well are we using our human resources—our volunteers, our staff, our board—as well as our financial resources? How do we know that? What should we be doing?

u. Are other/similar organizations doing a better job? If yes, why is that? What can we learn from them?

v. What have been the results of our efforts to attract and keep donors? What are our recruitment strengths? Our weaknesses? How do we know that?

w. How do we define and share our results with our donors? In what ways, if any, should we change our procedures? Why or why not?

5. What Is Our Plan?

On What Should We Be Focused?

Notes on Focus

a. What have we learned and what do we recommend? Why is that?

b. What are our performance strengths?
   (1) In the organization?
   (2) In my group/responsibility area?

c. What are the outside needs and opportunities that match our competencies and resources?

d. How well are we using our resources?

e. How can our strengths be exploited?

f. What, if anything, should we do differently?
   (1) Abandon or add programs? Why?
   (2) Address later? Why?
   (3) Outsource or refer to another organization? Why? Which programs or services? To whom?

5. What Is Our Plan? *(continued)*

What Are Our Priorities?

Notes on Priorities

a. What is the end result we want to achieve?

b. Will these decisions, policies, programs, activities advance our capacity to carry out our mission?

c. For each major program or activity, ask:
   (1) If we were not already doing this, if we were not already committed, would we start doing this now?
   (2) Is what we are doing still the right focus?

d. Which are the few things we can accomplish that will do the most for our organization (for my group)?
   (1) Short term (can we implement now/within twelve months)?
   (2) Long term (one year—three years)?

e. Which are the few things that either contribute marginally or are no longer of great significance?

f. What are the current priorities for our organization? For my specific group/responsibility area?

g. To what extent do they help fulfill the mission? The goals of the organization (or my group/responsibility area)?

h. To what extent are these priorities important? Are they "high" or "low" priorities? Why is that?

i. What other information or additional resources, if any, are needed?

5. What Is Our Plan? *(continued)*

**How Do We
Implement?**

Notes on
Implementation

a. What are the results we want to achieve?

b. What are our plans to achieve these results?
   (1) For my group/area?
   (2) For the organization?

c. What agreements have been reached/decisions made? What are our recommendations for:
   (1) Areas/decisions that still need to be addressed? Next steps?
   (2) Who bears responsibility for each task?
   (3) Correct timing?
   (4) Follow-up session?
   (5) How these agreements will be communicated and reported? To whom? When?

d. What are the next steps?

e. How do we implement?